MW01172436

THIS JOURNAL BELONGS TO:

Made in the USA
Middletown, DE
30 September 2023

39819963R00068